WALKING CLOSE TO

NORTH NORFOLK

Cromer and
Sheringham

Number Seventy in the popular series
of walking guides

ontents

alked, Written and Drawn by Clive Brown

Clive Brown 2011

lished by Clive Brown
N 978-1-907669-70-5

GW00383186

PLEASE
Take care of the countryside
Your leisure is someone's livelihood

Close gates
Start no fires
Keep away from livestock and animals
Do not stray from marked paths
Take litter home
Do not damage walls, hedgerows or fences
Cross only at stiles or gates
Protect plants, trees and wildlife
Keep dogs on leads
Respect crops, machinery and rural property
Do not contaminate water

Although not essential we recommend good walking boots; during hot weather ta▌ something to drink on the way. All walks can easily be negotiated by an averagel▌ fit person. The routes have been recently walked and surveyed, changes can however occur, please follow any signed diversions. Some paths cross fields whicl▌ are under cultivation. All distances and times are approximate.

The maps give an accurate portrayal of the area, but scale has however been sacrificed in some cases for the sake of clarity and to fit restrictions of page size.

Walking Close To have taken every care in the research and production of this gui▌ but cannot be held responsible for the safety of anyone using them.

During very wet weather, parts of these walks may become impassable through flooding, check before starting out. Stiles and rights of way can get overgrown during the summer; folding secateurs are a useful addition to a walker's rucksack.

Thanks to Angela for help in production of these booklets

Views or comments?
clive@walkingcloseto.com

7▌

Walking Close to North Norfolk
Cromer and Sheringham

high ground along the edge of the sea near Cromer, including Kelling Heath, is wn as the Cromer Ridge. It is a moraine consisting of the debris pushed along he end of the glacier grinding its way out of what is now the North Sea at the of the last Ice Age, ten thousand years ago. Parts of the coastline and cliffs subject to natural erosion and are very unstable and crumbling rapidly away into sea. The Department of the Environment has adopted a policy of 'Managed reat' leaving the coastline to evolve naturally.

mer developed from a fishing village to a holiday resort during the 19th century. t used as a summer retreat by the rich families of Norwich, the holiday business ; also greatly increased by the railway's arrival in 1887. Overstrand and Cromer) become more fashionable after a series of articles in the Daily Telegraph by the atre critic Clement Scott, who called the area Poppyland.

: present pier opened in 1901; in 1923 a lifeboat station was built on the end. : lifeboat was previously launched directly from the beach, a hazardous feat in ◄ weather.

early Victorian times the people of Lower Sheringham fished and the people of)er Sheringham farmed. The advent of the railway in 1887 encouraged the iside village to develop into today's holiday town. A handful of fishing boats still ?rate from the beach, but it is from the leisure market that Sheringham thrives.

:kling Hall, reputed to be the most haunted stately home in England, was built in early part of the 17th Century by Sir Henry Hobart. The estate had been owned nedieval times by Sir James Fastolf (1380-1459), who had been the inspiration Shakespeare's Falstaff. It was also the ancestral home of Anne Boleyn, whose er brother and sister were born there. The Hobarts became Earls of :kinghamshire but the 2nd Earl died childless and the estate passed through his igher's marriage to the Marquesses of Lothian. The estate became part of the tional trust after the death of the 11th Marquess in 1940. It spent the war years the officers mess for nearby RAF Oulton and was rented out to tenants before ng opened to the public in 1962.

: feel that it would be difficult to get lost with the instructions and map in this oklet, but recommend carrying an Ordnance Survey map. The walks are on olorer Map nos. 251 and 252; Landranger Map no 133 covers at a smaller scale. ads, geographical features and buildings, not on our map but visible from the lk can be easily identified.

1 Blakeney Eye

7 Miles $3^1/_4$ Hours

Use the car park at Wiveton Downs Local Nature Reserve on the minor road south west of Wiveton. No Facilities.

1 Go back towards the entrance, through the kissing gate and down to the road. Cross and go through the gate opposite and follow the path through the gorse to the far left corner. Cross the road and keep direction through the white gates, along the road between hedges and past the farm, all the way to the road.

2 Keep ahead on this tarmac driveway between hedges to the marker post at the junction of tracks and turn left along the field edge with the hedge to the right. Turn right at the end, downhill; follow the track right and immediate left along the field edge with the trees now left. Turn right in the corner and walk up to the far end. Turn left, around the bottom of the slope to the A149.

3 Turn right, carefully along this busy road for 40yds to the footpath signpost and take the track down to the T-junction with the coast path. Turn right and follow the path to the village sign at Blakeney Quay. Turn left along the quayside.

4 Take the Norfolk Coast Path to the left along the top of the embankment. Follow this track bearing right, with the marshes of Blakeney Eye to the right, all the way to the higher embankment near Cley Windmill and turn right along the top to the A149.

5 Cross carefully and turn right on the roadside path to the first junction. Take the road left to the T-junction and turn left to the crossroads at Wiveton. Keep straight on and turn immediate right, follow this road all the way back to the nature reserve car park and your vehicle.

Blakeney Point, the sand and shingle spit running for 10 miles mainly west of the village of Blakeney, is a haven for shore and sea birds. It is also a popular place to see Common or Grey Seals. Blakeney Point can be reached by a path from the village or a ferry from the harbour, the National Nature Reserve is closed during the breeding season.

The windmill at Cley was built in the early years of the 19th century; it worked until 1912 and was converted to a holiday home after the First World War. The mill was for over 70 years owned by the family of James Blunt the singer. It is presently offering bed and breakfast accommodation and wedding receptions.

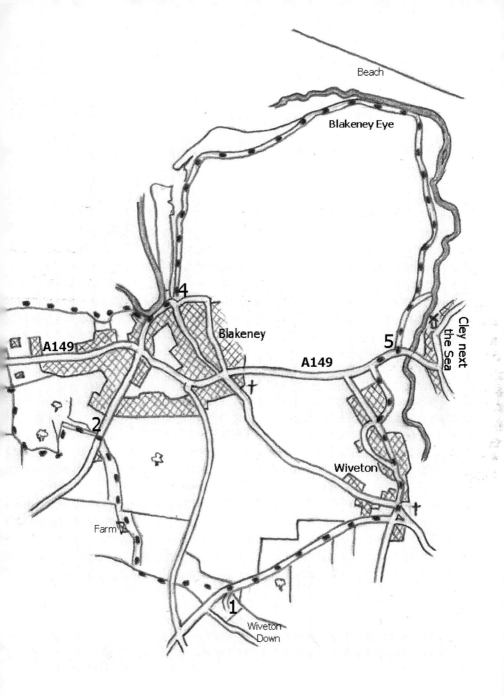

Beach

Blakeney Eye

4

Blakeney

A149

A149

5

Cley next
the Sea

2

Wiveton

Farm

Wiveton

1

Wiveton
Down

2 Holt Lowes

$5^1/_4$ Miles $2^1/_2$ Hours

Use the parking area at Mackay's Hill, off Hempstead Road south we
of Holt. No facilities.

1 Go past the wide wooden gate, away from the factories along the wide track
through the trees to a T-junction of paths at a marker post. Turn left, to the road
turn right and follow the road carefully into the dip and up the other side to the
signpost on the right.

2 Turn right, along the farm track with the hedge and the trees to the left; bear
right of a thicker growth of trees and left through a hedge gap. Bear further left
between the pond and the stream, cross the bridge and the adjacent stile; bear le
and step over the stile at the far end. Cross the next stile on the left and keep
ahead past the signpost, follow the tarmac drive left at the Hall and back to the
right. Carry on across the stream to the footbridge at the signpost on the right.

3 Cross and take the path with the stream to the right, carry on right and left,
past the church into Hempstead village. Keep ahead up Chapel Lane, all the way
the derestriction signs and turn right into the wide hedged right-of-way, Back Lane

4 Walk down to the road and turn right, back to the T-junction in the village.
Cross the road and keep ahead right, past the signpost and down the wide path.
Keep straight on, upslope across the field which may be under cultivation although
path should be well marked within any crop. Step over the stile at the end, follow
the field edge right and then left all the way to the barn.

5 Turn left to the end of the barn and join the more substantial farm track to the
right, continue downslope into the trees to the signpost at the grassy T-junction.
Turn left and go along the path between trees and then just trees to the left; follow
the path right, over the stream. Continue ahead through the trees and across the
field to the road at a signpost.

6 Take the track through the trees parallel to the road, past a stile at the end an
bear left to a marker post. Turn right, through the trees with a wire fence to the
left and the heathland of Holt Lowes to the right. At the end turn left through the
narrow gate, carry on for 115yds and turn right, into the dip. Follow the path left
and right, back to the car park and your vehicle.

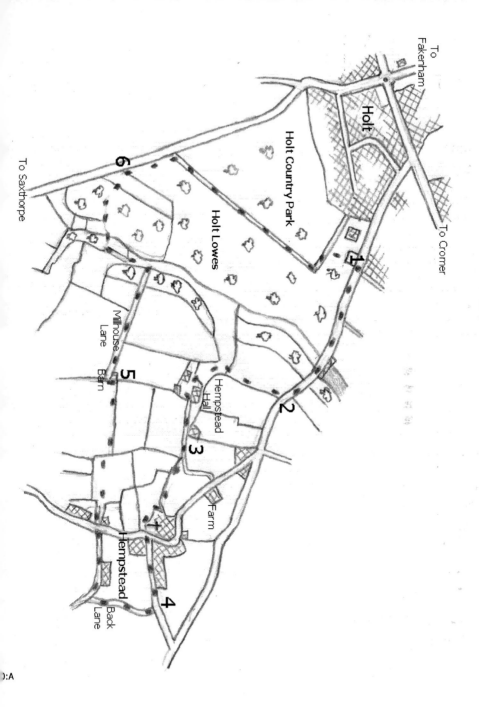

To Fakenham

Holt

To Cromer

Holt Country Park

Holt Lowes

To Saxthorpe

6

1

2

3

Millhouse Lane

5

Hempstead Hall

Farm

Hempstead

Back Lane

4

):A

3 Marble Hill

7 Miles $3^{1}/_{4}$ Hours

Find a parking space in Roughton. No toilets; local pub the 'New Inn' shop and post office at the garage, fish and chip shop/restaurant.

1 Start from the junction of the A140 with the B1436; take the roadside path of the B1436 towards Felbrigg, for two thirds of a mile to the junction. Turn left along Metton Road, out of the houses bearing right, uphill to the signpost.

2 Follow the wide track straight on, across the road and continue upslope through the gateway and into the trees at Marble Hill. Bear right at the junction of tracks and keep ahead to the Weavers' Way signpost in Felbrigg village.

3 Turn left along the wide track and go through the kissing gate, keep ahead over the grass and through the track at the trees to the narrow gate by the estate road at the corner of the trees. Turn left along the wide hardcore estate road, past the church to a T-junction of tracks.

4 Cross the field ahead, which may be under cultivation although a path should well marked within any crop, to the marker post in the corner at the trees. Follow the track through the trees to the marker post on the far side; keep direction along the field edge with the trees to the right, bearing right, to a signpost. Turn left across the field (a track should be visible); at the hedge step over both stiles and bear slight left to the stile/footbridge on the far side. Cross and keep ahead to the road in Metton.

5 Continue straight on up the track between hedges to a marker post, turn left and immediate right at the next marker post. Walk down the field edge with the hedge to the left, into the corner; turn right for 120yds to the steps.

6 Descend and follow the field edge ahead with the trees to the right, cross the stile at the bottom and bear right through the wide gap. Go along the right hand field edge bearing left across the stream and through the kissing gate. Bear left (a track should be visible) and go through the hedge gap on to the road.

7 Turn left to the T-junction and bear left with the road around a right hand bend to a sharp left corner. Just around the corner take the restricted byway upslope, bearing left on a narrower path down to Back Lane.

8 Turn right, to Roughton and take Old Turnpike Road to the left, leading back to the junction of the A140 and the B1436.

Felbrigg

3

Ibrigg Park

†

B1436

4

Marble
Hill

The Belt

2

A140

5

Metton

†

Back
Lane

6

Farm

7

8

Roughton

1

†

A140

70:A

4   Incleborough Hill

5$\frac{1}{2}$ Miles   2$\frac{1}{2}$ Hours

Find a parking space in Cromer, pay and display car parks all facilities available in the town. Start from the church.

1 Go towards the sea, down narrow Jetty Street to the railings overlooking the pier. Turn left along the path with the railing and the sea to the right. Bear right, down the concrete ramp to the beach and walk along the higher part of the beach for just over a mile to the concrete steps at East Runton Gap. (Check the tide, if it is going to get too high take the roadside path next to the A149, to the village.
2 Ascend the steps and keep ahead to the A149, turn right to the junction and le along Felbrigg Road; continue through the green and under both viaducts up to the pond on the right. Turn right with the pond to the left and bear left and right, alo the wide track, past the footpath signpost, with the flint wall to the right.
3 Follow the path between hedges and keep ahead at the junction with Incleborough Hill to the left, past a signpost. Continue up the narrow tarmac road with the trees to the right, to the junction. Take the narrower restricted byway to the right, with the bungalows to the right, up to the road.
4 Turn left to the National Trust Town Hill sign and take the path uphill over the summit and down to the junction of tracks. Turn left, past the white signpost alon the wider track. Go through a kissing gate and over an open piece of ground to a junction at a three way signpost.
5 Take the narrow path right, between trees, around corners to the road; cross and carry on under the railway and keep ahead between hedges. Continue ahead at the road junction along the narrow road between houses to the A148.
6 Turn left, back into Cromer to find your vehicle.

The North Norfolk Railway was completed in 1887 as part of the Eastern and Midlands Railway. Always financially insecure, a takeover by the Midland and Grea Northern Railways in 1893 made it part of a secondary line from Peterborough to Great Yarmouth. The line was never as busy as hoped and traffic decreased particularly during the 1930s. After the line became part of British Railways many people thought it would close quickly. Most of the line closed in 1959 but the part between Holt and Sheringham survived until the Beeching Axe of 1964. Enthusiast immediately set to work with a view to reopening the line as a tourist railway, whic was achieved in 1976 with lasting success.

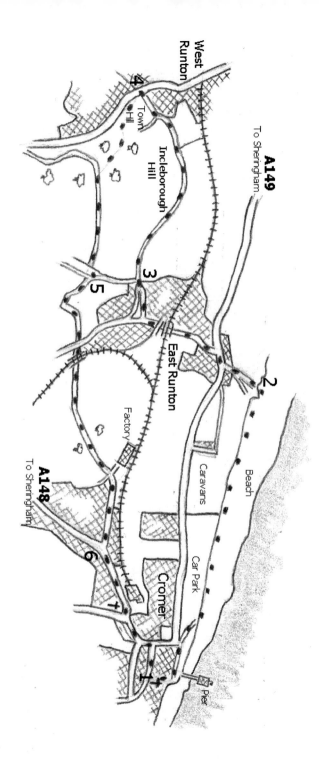

West Runton

A149
To Sheringham.

Town Hill

Incleborough Hill

3

5

East Runton

2

Factory

Caravans

Beach

A148
To Sheringham

6

Car Park

Cromer

1

Pier

5   Felbrigg Hall

$10^1/_4$ Miles $4^3/_4$ Hours

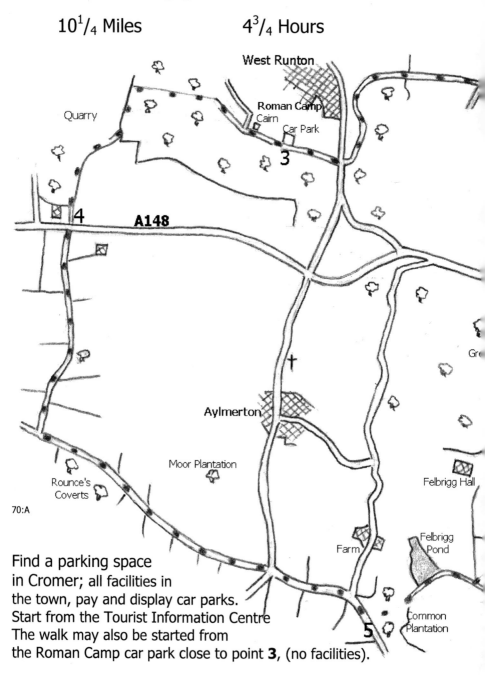

West Runton

Quarry

Roman Camp
Cairn
Car Park

3

4   **A148**

Aylmerton

Moor Plantation

Gr

Rounce's
Coverts

Felbrigg Hall

70:A

Farm

Felbrigg
Pond

Common
Plantation

5

Find a parking space
in Cromer; all facilities in
the town, pay and display car parks.
Start from the Tourist Information Centre
The walk may also be started from
the Roman Camp car park close to point **3**, (no facilities).

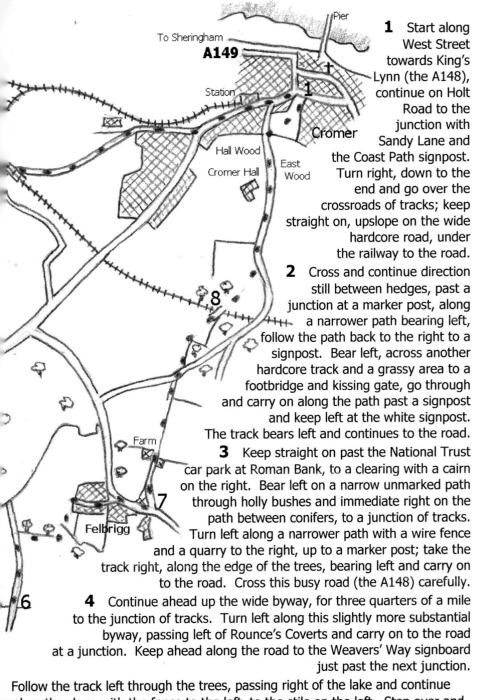

1 Start along West Street towards King's Lynn (the A148), continue on Holt Road to the junction with Sandy Lane and the Coast Path signpost. Turn right, down to the end and go over the crossroads of tracks; keep straight on, upslope on the wide hardcore road, under the railway to the road.

2 Cross and continue direction still between hedges, past a junction at a marker post, along a narrower path bearing left, follow the path back to the right to a signpost. Bear left, across another hardcore track and a grassy area to a footbridge and kissing gate, go through and carry on along the path past a signpost and keep left at the white signpost. The track bears left and continues to the road.

3 Keep straight on past the National Trust car park at Roman Bank, to a clearing with a cairn on the right. Bear left on a narrow unmarked path through holly bushes and immediate right on the path between conifers, to a junction of tracks. Turn left along a narrower path with a wire fence and a quarry to the right, up to a marker post; take the track right, along the edge of the trees, bearing left and carry on to the road. Cross this busy road (the A148) carefully.

4 Continue ahead up the wide byway, for three quarters of a mile to the junction of tracks. Turn left along this slightly more substantial byway, passing left of Rounce's Coverts and carry on to the road at a junction. Keep ahead along the road to the Weavers' Way signboard just past the next junction.

Follow the track left through the trees, passing right of the lake and continue ~ead up the slope with the fence to the left, to the stile on the left. Step over and

∞mpleted on the next Page (Fourteen)

follow the track in the grass to the church. Bear left at the wall, down to the gate and turn right, through the churchyard to the gate at the far corner, go through a turn right, down to the corner and go through the gate here.

6   Take the estate road left to the cattle grid and turn right, with the trees left, for 275yds; bear left through the trees and the kissing gate. Cross the field to the left hand end of the trees and carry on for 90yds to the kissing gate. Turn right along the driveway to the road in Felbrigg village; take the roadside path ahead to the Weavers' Way signpost.

7   Turn left, along the access road and continue straight on when the road ends, along the right hand field edge with the hedge to the right. Keep ahead through t hedged path to the road and turn right for 65yds to the steps on the left. Go up and bear slight right, along the field edge with the trees right. At the end, bear right, across a field which may be under cultivation although a path should be well marked within any crop.

8   Continue over the bridge across the railway line, through the field ahead and bear left at the corner, follow the track down to the road. Take the grass verge an path at the side of the road for two thirds of a mile to the signpost. Bear right through the playing field and go through the car park to the Tourist Information Centre on the far side.

---

6   The Quag

$4^1/_2$ Miles   2 Hours

Use the parking area signposted to the beach, off the A149 half a mile east of Salthouse. No facilities.

1 Go up to the top of the gravel embankment and turn right (east), past Gramborough Hill. After three quarters of a mile, close to the pill box on the beach turn right along the wide track between fences. Turn right, with The Quag lake to the left, to the T-junction of paths with the track Meadow Lane.

2 Turn left, up to the marker post for the permissive path on the right; take the path upslope with the trees to the right. In the corner turn left for 85yds and right at the marker post along the field edge to the far corner. Turn sharp left along the field edge parallel to the road, up to the marker post in the corner.

3 Cross the busy A149 carefully, go past the signpost, up the field edge with the hedge to the left and keep ahead between fields. Go through the hedge gap and continue with the hedge to the left up to the corner. Turn right, to the marker post in the hedge gap and take the wider track left, between hedges, to the road.

Keep straight on to the signpost on the right, go through the gap and cross the
[fiel]d on a left hand diagonal; this field may   be under cultivation although a
[trac]k should be visible within any crop.

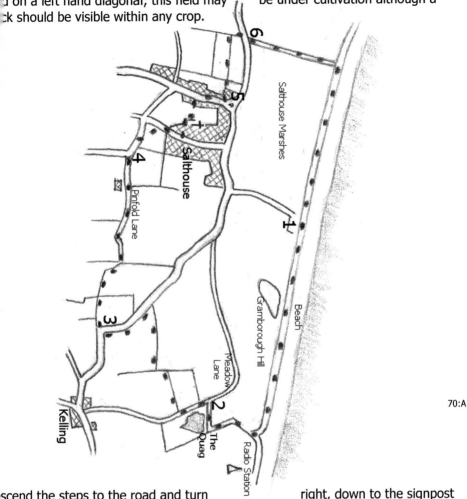

70:A

[De]scend the steps to the road and turn   right, down to the signpost
[on] the left to the church. Turn left, follow the path right and left and go through
[the] churchyard left of the church; carry on along the narrow path to the road. Turn
[rig]ht, down to the signpost on the left just before the A149.

Go through wooden barriers and the kissing gate, continue up the right hand
[fie]ld edge and go through the next kissing gate. Cross the field which may be under
[cul]tivation (a track should be visible) and carry on with the hedge to the right. Go
[do]wnslope on the narrow path between hedges and bear right to the A149.

Cross carefully and take the track ahead through the marshes to the gravel
[em]bankment. Turn right for two thirds of a mile, back to the car park and your
[ve]hicle.

7 Fox Hills

4³/₄ Miles   2¹/₄ Hours

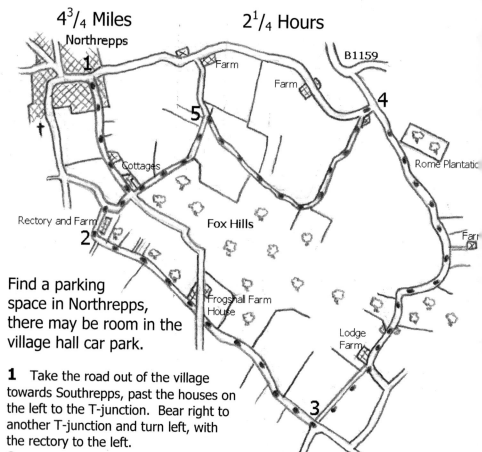

Find a parking
space in Northrepps,
there may be room in the
village hall car park.

1 Take the road out of the village
towards Southrepps, past the houses on
the left to the T-junction. Bear right to
another T-junction and turn left, with
the rectory to the left.

2 Follow the track left and keep ahead between trees; cross the road and
continue with the trees to the left all the way to the road at the white gates.

3 Take the path left, past the signpost along the field edge with the hedge to the
left and join the road left/straight on. Carry on along this road for a mile and a
quarter to the T-junction close to the main junction.

4 Turn left for 85yds to the narrow unsigned path on the left, take the path all the
way to the trees at the end and follow the path right with the trees of Fox Hills to
the left. Continue between fields to a marker post at a junction of tracks.

5 Turn Sharp left along this path to the marker post at the corner at the trees and
bear right along the path with the trees to the left, down to the road. Take the road
left back to Northrepps and your vehicle.

Kelling Heath

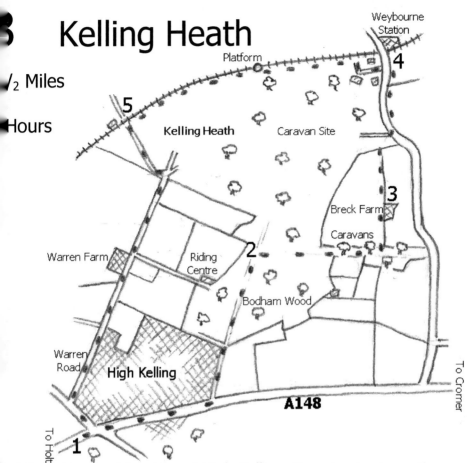

/2 Miles

Hours

art from the road junction at High Kelling; there is a lay-by on the
estbound side of the A148, west of the junction. No facilities.

Take the roadside path towards Cromer, where the houses end turn left down
e path between the fence and the trees. Continue past the wooden barrier and
e Forestry Commission sign along a wider track between trees, carry on over two
ossroads of tracks; the path turns slight right and then left to a T-junction.

Turn right, over a crossroads in a dip and back upslope; carry on along the wide
ack in the narrow belt of trees. Just before a tree on the right marked by discs,
rn left through the trees and keep ahead on the right hand field edge, past the
ravans and Breck Farm.

Continue parallel to the telegraph poles and bear right on the path through the
es to the junction at the entrance to the caravan site. Take the path in the gully,
wnslope parallel to the road, to the entrance to Springs Farm.

mpleted on the next Page (Eighteen)

4 Turn left, down the driveway and the narrower path between fences, bearing right to the railway. Carry on along the path parallel to the railway, passing over the station platform; the path continues close to the railway along the top of the cutting to the white crossing gates.

5 Take the wide track left through Kelling Heath, bearing left to a marker post with yellow discs. Turn right, past wooden barriers and walk along the narrow pat between the trees and the hedge, keep direction past Warren Farm on a concrete then gravel driveway to the road. Turn left back to the junction with the A148.

9 Blickling Park

5^1/$_2$ Miles   2^1/$_2$ Hours

Use the car park at Blickling Hall (National Trust), pay and display; toilets, shop and other facilities.

1 Go out of the back of the car park on to the estate road and turn left past the signpost at the tree seat, bear right through the gate into Blickling Park and bear left at the fork on the hardcore estate road between fences. Follow this obvious track past the trees all the way to the parking area.

2 Turn left from the car park entrance along the narrow tarmac road to Itteringham Common village. Turn right at the signpost at the junction and cross the footbridge ahead, turn immediate right across the next footbridge and bear lef up the slight slope. Step over the stile and keep direction up the right hand field edge with the hedge to the right, at the top corner bear right, through the gate.

3 Keep ahead up the narrow field and cross the stile on the right, continue upslope on the right hand field edge with the hedge to the right, through the hedg at the end and continue with Brickkiln Plantation then the hedge to the left. Follow the track right and left and keep ahead past the farm, along the hardcore road between fields. Go through the gate and turn left/straight on past Fring Wood, bearing right, into the corner.

4 As the road swings left keep straight on along the wide footpath between hedges. At the marker post keep direction on the field edge with the hedge now right and follow this field edge left to the stile. Cross and keep ahead with the hedge now left, down to the River Bure and cross over the footbridge. Carry on ahead over the next footbridge and follow the boardwalk to the road.

Turn right for 80yds to the signpost and take the path left, (it is often easier to ollow the right hand field edge). Continue ahead on a slight upslope with the trees the left and carry on through the trees. Keep direction on the hardcore road tween fences through Blickling Park, back to the car park and your vehicle.

10   Baconsthorpe Castle

5 Miles $2^1/_2$ Hours

Use the small parking area close to the playing field on the eastern section of Church Lane. There is also a car park at the castle. No facilities.

1   Leave the car park entrance along the road to the left and walk up to the crossroads. Turn right up Long Lane to the T-junction and right for 70yds to the footpath signpost.

2   Take the driveway to the left. Go up the field edge with the hedge to the left and follow this track left and right, into the bottom corner. Turn right, still in this same field to the corner and turn left over the stile. Carry on ahead with the hedge and the dyke to the left, over the footbridge and continue with the hedge now righ Cross the stile footbridge on to the concrete farm road and turn left to the castle.

3   Go past the entrance and turn left, along the wide grassy track with the hedge to the right, bear right with the track and then left down to the road. Turn left an immediate right, walk up this field edge with the hedge to the right, into the corne

4   Turn left, across a farm track at a marker post, keep ahead with the hedge stil right and join the narrow tree lined path to the road. Turn left for 35yds and take the bridleway past the signpost; bear left up the tree lined track past the cottage t a T-junction of tracks.

5   Turn right, past Broomhill Farm; the path narrows as it bears left through tree and bears right along a right hand field edge with trees to the right, down to the road. Turn left for 400yds to the signpost on the left.

6   Take the wide track, Harp Lane, to the left between trees. Cross the road and keep ahead into the farm entrance; continue bearing left of the house, through a gate. Keep direction on left hand field edges to the road at a corner.

7   Turn left and follow this road back to the crossroads in Baconsthorpe. Keep ahead back to the car park and your vehicle.

Baconsthorpe Castle, actually the ruins of a fortified Manor House, was built during the late 15th century by the Haydon family. Sir John Haydon had made a fortune as a lawyer; his immediate successors made a second fortune from the wo trade. Part of the castle was used for the production of cloth, which was exported to the Netherlands. Money ebbed away from the family, now known as Haydens, during the 17th century and they began to sell off parts of the castle as building material. By the end of the Civil War, only the gatehouse was left; this continued t

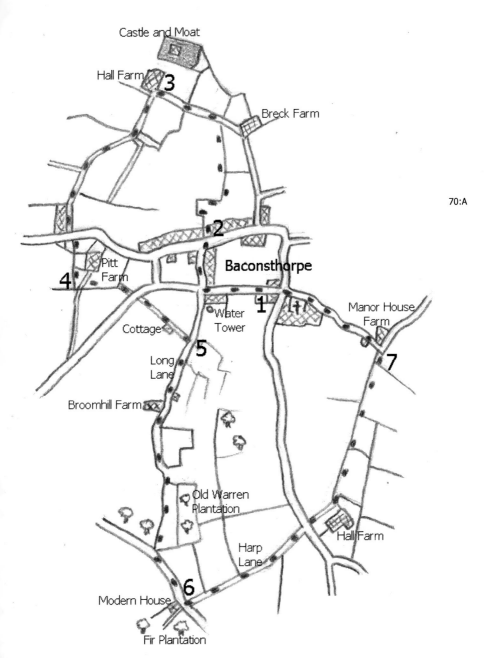

Castle and Moat

Hall Farm **3**

Breck Farm

70:A

2

Pitt Farm

Baconsthorpe

4

Cottage

Water Tower

1

Manor House Farm

7

Long Lane

5

Broomhill Farm

Old Warren Plantation

Hall Farm

Harp Lane

Modern House **6**

Fir Plantation

used until a partial collapse in 1920. The surviving ruins are now looked after by ̣lish Heritage.

11   Sheringham Common

$4^1/_4$ Miles   2 Hours

Use the lay-by on the eastbound side of the A148, half a mile east of the A1082 turn to Sheringham, signposted to 'Hilltop' and recycling. No facilities.

1   Walk along the lay-by to the west, west of the 'Hilltop gate', towards Holt, to the kissing gate on the right. Go through and take the path through the trees parallel to the road, to a marker post and turn right, downslope on a narrow path between low embankments. Keep parallel to a more substantial path coming in from the right, to a wider hardcore track.

2   Cross and keep ahead slight left, along the bottom of the valley; bearing left upslope to the houses and the Anglian Water plant. Keep direction along the edge of Sheringham Common with the hedge and the houses to the left. At a marker post, bear right to a fence and turn right across a concrete footbridge.

3   Keep ahead bearing left at the pond and carry on down to the road, cross and go over the grassy area to the road at the houses. Turn right, up to Church Lane and left down to the railway; take the path right, along the foot of the embankment and past the allotments.

4   Follow the wide track right, back to the A149; turn left and bear immediate right through wooden gates. Go past the Coast Path marker post and turn right, along the farm road past the school and Hall Farm; continue upslope between walls then hedges to the signpost at the treeline.

5   Keep ahead/right uphill on a narrower path over a crossroads of paths at the crest. Maintain direction through trees to a fork just before a large Norfolk Heritage yellow marker disc on a tree. Take the left fork and bear left at the marker post, along the path with the fence to the right.

6   At the end, bear right, between trees with the open field to the left. About 180yds short of the A148, turn right on a narrow path through trees to the road. Turn left to the main road and take the wide grass verge to the right, back to the lay-by and your vehicle.

The Felbrigg name originated in the 12th century with Sir Simon de Felbrigg who was a courtier of King Richard I. The estate was owned for over 250 years by the Wyndham family who built the present house during the early 17th century. Robert Wyndham Ketton-Cremer, who was a distant ancestor of the last Wyndham, was the final owner; he died childless in 1969 and left the house to the National Trust.

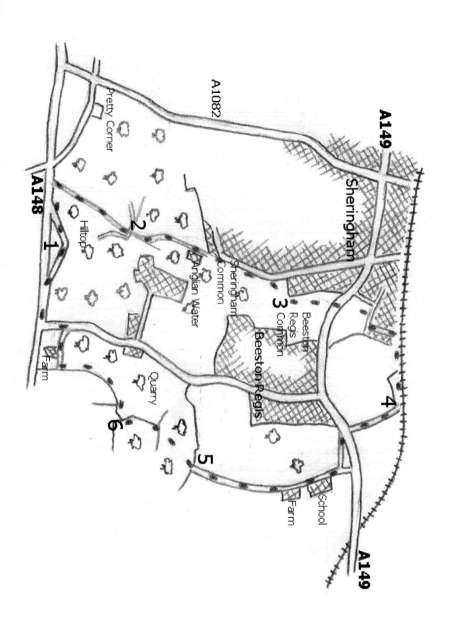

A148

A1082

A149

Pretty Corner

Sheringham

Hilltop

1

2

Sheringham Common

Anglian Water

Beeston Regis Common

3

Beeston Regis

4

Farm

Quarry

6

5

Farm

School

A149

The 'Walking Close to' Series

Peterborough
The Nene near Peterborough
The Nene Valley Railway near Wansford
The Nene near Oundle
The Torpel Way (Peterborough to Stamford)
The Great North Road near Stilton

Cambridge
Grafham Water (Huntingdonshire)
The Great Ouse in Huntingdonshire
The Cam and the Granta near Cambridge
Newmarket

Northamptonshire
The Nene near Thrapston
The Nene near Wellingborough
The River Ise near Kettering
The Nene near Northampton
Pitsford Water
Rockingham Forest
Daventry and North West Northamptonshire

Leicestershire
Rutland Water
Eye Brook near Uppingham
The Soar near Leicester
Lutterworth
The Vale of Belvoir (North Leicestershire)
Melton Mowbray
The Welland near Market Harborough

Lincolnshire
The Welland near Stamford
Bourne and the Deepings
South Lincolnshire

Suffolk
Lavenham in Suffolk
Bury St Edmunds
The Stour near Sudbury
The Orwell near Ipswich
Dedham Vale
Stowmarket
Clare, Cavendish and Haverhill

Essex/Hertfordshire
Hertford and the Lee Valley
The Colne near Colchester
Epping Forest (North London)
Chelmsford
Saffron Walden (2011)

Warwickshire
Rugby

Wiltshire/Bath
The Avon near Bath
Bradford-on-Avon
Corsham and Box
The Avon near Chippenham

Bedfordshire/Milton Keynes
The Great Ouse near Bedford
The Great Ouse North of Milton Keynes
Woburn Abbey

Somerset & Devon
Cheddar Gorge
Glastonbury and the City of Wells
The Quantock Hills
The East Devon Coast (Sidmouth, Branscombe and Beer)
Exmouth (East Devon) (2011)

Norfolk
The Norfolk Broads (Northern Area)
The Norfolk Broads (Southern Area)
The Great Ouse near King's Lynn
North West Norfolk (Hunstanton and Wells)
Thetford Forest
North Norfolk (Cromer and Sheringham)

Nottinghamshire
Sherwood Forest
The Dukeries (Sherwood Forest)
The Trent near Nottingham

Oxfordshire
The Thames near Oxford
The Cotswolds near Witney
The Vale of White Horse
Woodstock and Blenheim Palace
Henley-on-Thames
Banbury

Worcester/Hereford
The Severn near Worcester
South West Herefordshire (Kington and Hay-on-Wye)

Cumbria
Cartmel and Southern Lakeland